MAURICE RICHARD

PATRICK ROY

HOWIE MORENZ

JOSÉ THÉODORE

HECTOR BLAKE

JEAN BÉLIVEAU

OLEG PETROV

BOB GAINEY

GUY LAPOINTE

SAKU KOIVU

GUY LAFLEUR

GEORGES VEZINA

The History of the

MONTREAL
CANADIENS

Michael E. Goodman

CREATIVE C EDUCATION

Published by Creative Education, 123 South Broad Street, Mankato, MN 56001

Creative Education is an imprint of The Creative Company.

Designed by Rita Marshall.

Photographs by Getty Images (Al Bello/Allsport, Jeff Gross/NHLI, Harry How/NHLI,

John F. Jaqua/Time Life Pictures, Craig Melvin/NHLI, Dave Sanford/NHLI) Hockey Hall of Fame

(Paul Bereswill, Imperial Oil-Turofsky, London Life-Portnoy, Dave Sandford),

Icon Sports Media, Inc., SportsChrome USA (Gregg Forwerck, Craig Melvin)

Library of Congress Cataloging-in-Publication Data

Goodman, Michael E. The history of the Montreal Canadiens / by Michael Goodman.

p. cm. — (Stanley Cup champions)   ISBN 1-58341-273-5

Summary: Presents the history, players, and accomplishments of

the famous Montreal Canadiens.

1. Montreal Canadiens (Hockey team)—History—Juvenile literature.

[1. Montreal Canadiens (Hockey team)—History. 2. Hockey—History.] I. Title. II. Series.

GV848.M6 G66 2003   796.962'64'0971428—dc21   2002034877

First Edition 9 8 7 6 5 4 3 2 1

IN THE 1600s, MANY FRENCH COLONISTS SETTLED IN NEW FRANCE, AN AREA THAT IS NOW THE CANADIAN PROVINCE OF QUEBEC. THESE COLONISTS WERE SOMETIMES called *les habitants*, French for "the inhabitants." The largest and most important settlement occupied by *les habitants* was Montreal, located on the St. Lawrence River. Even when New France came under British control in 1760, most Montreal citizens continued to speak French.

By the early 1900s, hockey had become the most popular sport in Montreal and the rest of Canada. But most of the city's professional teams represented Montreal's English community, and the city's French majority clamored for a team of its own. That franchise, called the Club de Hockey Canadien, was finally formed in December 1909. Although officially known as the Canadiens, the team was nicknamed "Les Habitants," or "Habs" for short.

GEORGES VEZINA

{FIRST CUPS} The Canadiens played their first games on an outdoor rink called the Jubilee, and Montreal's enthusiastic fans

In **1919–20**, the Canadiens averaged 5.38 goals per game, a franchise record that still stands.

often braved below-zero temperatures to watch their new heroes. The club's offense was led in those early years by wing Jack Laviolette and center Edouard "Newsy" Lalonde, and the nets were guarded by legendary goaltender Georges Vezina, one of hockey's most dominant players. Vezina was so great that, in his honor, the National Hockey League (NHL) today honors the best goaltender each year with the Vezina Trophy.

The all-French club had some early success, but the team really began to excel once it permitted top English-speaking players to join in 1915. The next season, the bi-lingual Canadiens won the National Hockey Association title (the NHL was not formed until 1917) and defeated the Portland Rosebuds of the Pacific Coast

PATRICE BRISEBOIS

An NHL legend, Howie Morenz led Montreal in goals for seven straight seasons.

HOWIE MORENZ

Hockey Association in a special playoff to win their first Stanley

Cup—the big silver chalice awarded to the world champion. Each

Canadiens player received $238 as victory pay.

The Canadiens did not win a second Cup until

eight years later, in 1924. By that time, the club was

led by its first true superstar, Howie Morenz from

Stratford, Ontario. Morenz, who was known as the

Tough winger Billy Boucher was the NHL's most penalized player in **1922–23** and **1924–25**.

"Stratford Streak," had blazing speed and a powerful shot. "His

speed was incredible," said Toronto Maple Leafs defenseman King

Clancy. "Morenz would pick up the puck behind his own net and in

two strides would be at top speed, which was the closest thing to

flying I've seen. He was very difficult to stop."

In Montreal's 1923 training camp, Morenz won a spot at center

between high-scoring wings Auriel Joliat and Billy Boucher. He

scored a goal in his NHL debut in December 1923, and by the time

BILLY BOUCHER

DOUG GILMOUR

the season was over, Morenz had propelled the Canadiens to their second Stanley Cup. But that was just the beginning. Morenz played

In one **1943** game, the Canadiens exploded for a team-record 35 points (goals plus assists).

10 seasons in Montreal, leading the Habs to the Cup two more times (in 1930 and 1931) and earning three Hart Trophies as the NHL's Most Valuable Player. He helped make the Canadiens' new home, an arena called the Forum, the center of the hockey world.

The Great Depression hurt Canadian hockey in the 1930s, especially in Montreal. The city's English-speaking NHL team, the Maroons, folded in 1938, while the Canadiens barely managed to survive financially. The Habs struggled in the league standings, too. They would not bring home another Stanley Cup until 1944, once a high-flying "rocket" had soared onto the scene.

{THE ROCKET'S GLARE} Maurice "Rocket" Richard, a star wing for the Canadiens for 18 seasons (1942–60), was often called

MAURICE RICHARD

the "Babe Ruth of hockey." Like the Babe, Richard was a flamboyant

offensive standout who helped turn his team into a dynasty. During

Richard's years in Montreal, the Canadiens won eight regular-season

championships (with the league's best record) and captured eight

Stanley Cups, including five in a row from 1956 to 1960.

When Babe Ruth hit 60 home runs during the 1927 season, he

astounded the sports world. Richard's 50 goals in 50 games during

the 1944–45 season was just as remarkable a feat. It would be 36

Doug Harvey won the Norris Trophy (NHL's best defenseman) six times in the **1950s** and **'60s**.

years before another NHL player (winger Mike Bossy

of the New York Islanders) scored that many goals

that quickly. In 1958, Richard became hockey's first

600-goal scorer (playoff goals included). A reporter

once asked him which goals he remembered most

vividly. "The only goals I remember are ones that win games for the

Canadiens," Rocket replied.

Richard teamed with left wing Hector "Toe" Blake and center

Elmer Lach to form the "Punch Line," the most potent scoring trio in

the NHL in the 1940s. But they were just three of the standouts on

the Canadiens roster. The Habs also featured goaltender Bill Durnan

and defenseman Emile "Butch" Bouchard. That group won the

Stanley Cup in 1944 and 1946 and reached the Cup Finals in 1947.

RICHARD ZEDNICK

Eventually, all five would be elected to the Hockey Hall of Fame.

Although Richard set numerous scoring records during his

career, he never won a season points scoring title. He came closest

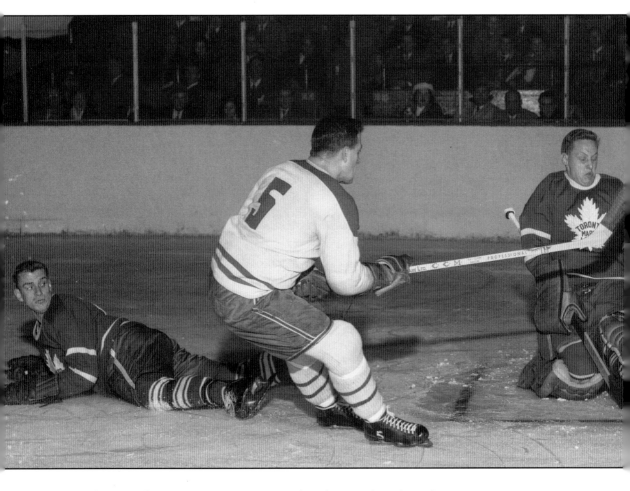

during the 1954–55 season. Richard was ahead in the scoring race

with four games left when he got involved in a brawl and was sus-

pended for the rest of the season. Teammate Bernard "Boom Boom"

Geoffrion ended up passing Richard in points. Montreal fans were

angry that NHL Commissioner Clarence Campbell had suspended

Richard. They rioted during the last game of the

season, damaging the Forum and destroying much of

downtown Montreal. Peace was restored only when

Richard went on the radio and begged fans to stop

the destruction.

In **1960–61**, wing Bernard Geoffrion became just the second NHL player to score 50 goals in a season.

{A DYNAMIC DYNASTY} Things were peaceful outside the

Forum as the 1955–56 season opened, but the excitement inside the

building was just starting. The Habs were about to begin one of the

most remarkable runs in NHL history.

New coach Toe Blake had assembled a star-studded lineup

that included his old line mate, Rocket Richard; Rocket's brother

Henri Richard and fellow center Jean Béliveau; wingers Boom Boom

Geoffrion and Dickie Moore; defensemen Doug Harvey and

B. GEOFFRION

Like the great Hector Blake, Oleg Petrov was a small but versatile Montreal winger.

Tom Johnson; and goalie Jacques Plante. All of these players were

future Hall-of-Famers. This powerful Canadiens team won five

Jean Béliveau (left) finished his amazing Canadiens career with 507 goals and 712 assists.

straight Stanley Cups from 1956 to 1960, when the

Rocket retired. Then, led by the 6-foot-4 Béliveau, the

Habs captured five more Cups in the seven seasons

between 1965 and 1971.

Montreal was so dominant that it caused the NHL

to make a rules change. Prior to the 1950s, players assessed a minor

penalty had to sit out a full two minutes in the penalty box. The

Canadiens' power play was so effective, however, that Montreal

could routinely score two or three goals during a two-minute

penalty and put the game out of reach. To keep games closer and

more competitive, the NHL decided that a player serving a minor

penalty could return to the game if a goal was scored against his

team—a rule that still stands today.

JEAN BÉLIVEAU

Throughout these glory years, Béliveau served as the team's

captain and offensive leader. His unselfish playmaking ability helped

turn several talented young wings—such as Gilles Tremblay and

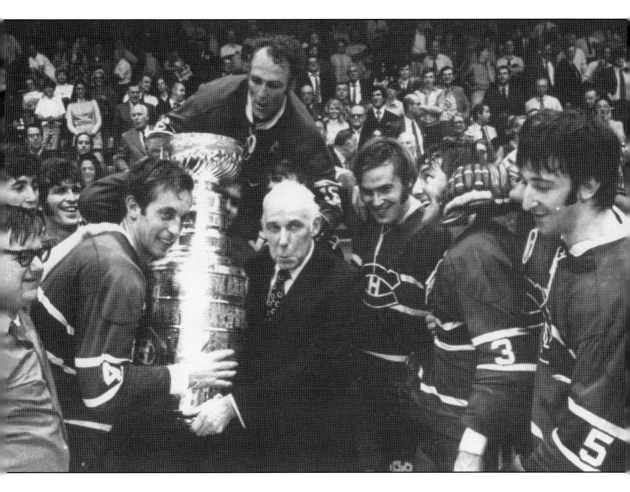

Yvan Cournoyer—into solid scorers. "The key to everything is my

skating," Béliveau once explained. "As a center, I have to be first

when we hit the blue line. If I'm a half-step slow, my passes will be intercepted or the wingers will be thrown offside."

Even after he retired as a player, Béliveau continued to lead

During the **1974–75** season, Guy Lapointe netted 28 goals, a franchise record for defensemen.

the Canadiens to victory as a team executive. In all, he

was part of 17 Stanley Cup-winning teams in

Montreal—10 as a player and 7 as an executive.

{FLOWER POWER} In June 1971, the day after

Béliveau announced his retirement, the Canadiens

drafted their next superstar, a flashy wing named Guy Lafleur. In

French, Lafleur means "the flower," and the new star helped launch

an era in Montreal known as "Flower Power."

Lafleur got off to a slow start in Montreal. Then, during the

1974–75 season, his fourth as a pro, Lafleur decided to take off his

helmet and let his long blond hair blow freely as he raced up and

down the ice. The new look seemed to inspire his play as well, and

he scored more than 100 points (goals plus assists) in a season for

GUY LAPOINTE

A two-time NHL Most Valuable Player, Guy Lafleur was a dominant of-fensive force.

GUY LAFLEUR

the first time. The next season, Lafleur won his first NHL scoring title and led the Habs to another Stanley Cup. Over the next three years, Lafleur earned two more scoring titles, and the Canadiens claimed all three Cup championships.

The game's best defensive wing in the late **1970s**, Bob Gainey helped build a Montreal dynasty.

Many Montreal fans believe that the Flower Power squad—which featured a first line of Lafleur, huge center Peter Mahovlich, and hard-as-nails winger Steve Shutt; defensive forward supreme Bob Gainey; defensemen Serge Savard, Guy Lapointe, and Larry Robinson; and acrobatic goalie Ken Dryden—was the best Canadiens squad of all time. Some experts believe it may have been the greatest NHL squad of all time. "The 1975–76 and 1976–77 Canadiens teams may have been the best ever in the NHL," said Don Cherry, who coached the Boston Bruins during those years. "They were even better than the 1980s [Edmonton] Oilers because of the defense."

BOB GAINEY

{A KING IN GOAL} The 1980s were dominated by the New

York Islanders and Edmonton Oilers. Still, the Canadiens main-

tained a high level of play throughout the decade, winning five

division titles and reaching the Stanley Cup Finals twice. In the

1986 playoffs, the Habs relied on rookie goalie Patrick Roy to

defeat the Calgary Flames and win the club's 23rd Stanley Cup.

Roy, whose name is pronounced *ruh-WA* and means "king" in French, had a solid but unspectacular regular season in 1985–86. But the rookie came up big in the playoffs. Roy was in goal for all 20 Montreal contests, won 15 of them, and allowed opponents fewer than two goals per game. After the Canadiens defeated the Flames in the finals in five games, Roy was awarded the Conn Smythe Trophy as the Most Valuable Player of the playoffs.

Patrick Roy played 665 games for Montreal, more than any other Canadiens goaltender.

Roy was even more impressive the next time the Canadiens won the Cup, in 1993. He was in the nets for all 16 Montreal post-season victories, including 10 contests that went into sudden-death overtime. Roy faced 65 shots during those overtime periods and turned away every one. "My concentration was at such a high level," Roy told a *Sports Illustrated* reporter. "My mind was right there. I felt fresh, like I could stop everything."

PATRICK ROY

Unfortunately, following the 1993 Cup triumph, Montreal's

fortunes began to turn. Roy suffered an appendicitis attack in the first

Center Vincent
Damphousse
was the team's
top assists
man in
1992–93,
1993–94, and
1994–95.

round of the 1994 playoffs, and the Canadiens were

quickly eliminated by the Boston Bruins. The following

season, the club failed to make the playoffs for the first

time in 25 years. Much of the blame was placed on

Roy, and he began to feud with team management.

When he was left in the nets in a December 1995 blowout in

which he gave up nine goals, an embarrassed Roy demanded to be

traded. Four days later he was sent to the Colorado Avalanche. Roy

led his new team to the Stanley Cup in 1996 and by 2001 would

become the NHL's all-time victory leader among goalies.

{A PERIOD OF REBUILDING} Roy's departure was just the

beginning of an era of change in Montreal. The Habs moved into a

new home, the Molson Centre, in March 1996 and began a slow

V. DAMPHOUSSE

rebuilding process. Montreal fans, accustomed to cheering for a contender, grew impatient when the club failed to make the playoffs in 1999, 2000, and 2001.

By the 2001–02 season, the Canadiens were led by a new coach, Michel Therrien, and a new star, goaltender José Théodore. Théodore carried the Habs back to the playoffs in 2002 by leading all NHL goalies during the regular season with a sensational .931 save percentage. For his efforts, Théodore was awarded both the Vezina Trophy and the Hart Trophy, becoming the first Montreal player to win the Hart Trophy since Guy Lafleur in 1978. "Lafleur was one of my idols," said Théodore. "I'm very happy to be a Montreal Canadien right now."

Canadiens fans were also happy to cheer for Théodore and his supporting cast, which included Finnish center and team captain

Steady wing Martin Rucinsky represented the Canadiens in the **2000** NHL All-Star Game.

MARTIN RUCINSKY

A small but fierce center, Saku Koivu hoped to lead Montreal up the NHL standings.

SAKU KOIVU

José Théodore reminded Montreal fans of such goal-tender greats as Georges Vezina.

JOSÉ THÉODORE

Saku Koivu; talented playmakers Yanik Perreualt and Joe Juneau at center; veteran wings Richard Zednik and Oleg Petrov; and solid

European winger Jan Bulis appeared ready to become a big part of the Montreal offense.

defenseman Patrice Brisebois. Fans were confident that the club's return to playoff contention signaled the beginning of a new era of winning hockey in Montreal.

The Canadiens have come a long way since their early days on a frigid outdoor rink. Over the years, "Les Habitants" have united both French-speaking and English-speaking Canadians who take pride in rooting for hockey's most successful franchise. Today's team plans to continue the club's winning tradition and leave its own mark on Canadiens history.

JAN BULIS